The ULTIMATE
skinny
mini
COOKBOOK

The ULTIMATE
skinny mini
COOKBOOK

---

one & done
DINNERS, DESSERTS, AND OTHER DELIGHTS

© 2016 Castle Point Publishing

All rights reserved. No portion of this book may be reproduced or transmitted in any form or by any means, electronic or mechanical, including photocopying, recording, and other information storage and retrieval systems, without prior written permission of the publisher.

Cover and interior design by Katie Jennings Campbell

Castle Point Publishing
58 Ninth Street
Hoboken, NJ 07030
www.castlepointpub.com

ISBN: 978-0-9981043-0-0

Please note: Read the safety instructions that came with your Skinny Mini or other rice cooker before trying any of the recipes in this book. The author, publisher, manufacturer, nor distributor can assume responsibility for the effectiveness of the recipes or text herein and shall have no liability for damages (whether direct, indirect, consequential, or otherwise) arising from the use, attempted use, misuse, or application of the directions described in this book.

Printed and bound in the United States of America

10 9 8 7 6 5 4 3 2 1

contents

introduction

TO ME, COOKING IS LOVE, and the Skinny Mini cooker holds a special place in my heart. It's small, yet bountiful. It's useful for college students who are trying to make a quick and filling dinner, grandparents making omelets for their grandkids, and everyone in between. It's super easy to use, yet can make dishes full of complex flavors.

In *The Ultimate Skinny Mini Cookbook*, you'll find recipes that not only showcase the many different kinds of food the Skinny Mini can make, but also the wide variety of meals you can create with similar ingredients. Latin food is so much more than shrimp tacos and cilantro rice (though those appear here as well!): it's a melting pot of many different flavors and cultures. So in addition to Latin-inspired dishes like vegetable timbale and chicken enchiladas, you'll find classics you'll remember from your own childhood like creamy mac 'n' cheese and pineapple upside-down cake, along with new favorites like cauliflower "rice" and noodles made from zucchini. (For all of these recipes and more, check out the Index in the back of the book.)

First, I'll give you a few easy breakfasts you can make in the Skinny Mini, from oatmeal to omelets (and did you know you can make an easy jam, too?). After some tasty appetizers including my favorite—salsa verde—you'll find creative side dishes. You probably knew the Skinny Mini could make delicious rice, but how about coconut rice with cashews? Or, go beyond rice and try couscous, polenta, quinoa, or vegetable dishes like creamed spinach or edamame and corn succotash. In the Easy Soups and Sandwiches chapter, you'll find just that, including an easy French onion soup and a mouthwatering Philly cheesesteak sandwich. Next, I'll give you more than a dozen delicious dinners, many of which use the Skinny Mini's steamer insert to perfectly cook Peruvian-style whitefish, lemon butter tilapia, Asian-inspired salmon, and more. And if you didn't know you could easily make meatloaf in the Skinny Mini, you're in for a treat.

Finally, who could forget the desserts? In the final chapter, you'll find my favorite cakes, brownies, and bread pudding along with some classy poached fruit, and more. Plus, I share some delicious beverages like white chocolate–peppermint hot chocolate and an amazingly simple way to make horchata.

No matter what the recipe, I've made sure there are no long lists of ingredients, and of course, it's all as easy as One and Done! Most recipes are as simple as setting the Skinny Mini to Cook and just walking away. That's why it's one of the most easy-to-use kitchen appliances out there. Set it, then get your kids ready for bed, make dessert while you're eating dinner, or keep your hors d'oeuvres warm while you're entertaining your guests! With its Keep Warm feature, the Skinny Mini is even great for serving both cheese and chocolate fondue!

The Skinny Mini is so simple to use, you'll find that experimenting with foods you might not have eaten before is easier than ever! I hope this inspiring cookbook gives you a few ideas that become the favorite meals you love for a lifetime.

—**Lorena Garcia**

bountiful breakfasts

Begin your morning the easy (and delicious!) way with these versatile breakfast recipes. Add your favorite berries to oatmeal, make an omelet without having to babysit a pan, and even prepare fruit jam without any canning equipment. Just plug in the Skinny Mini when you wake up and breakfast will be ready to go by the time you're out of your pajamas.

bright 'n' early blueberry oatmeal

Having a warm breakfast couldn't be easier with this simply perfect blueberry oatmeal recipe. Add a touch of lemon zest to brighten the blueberries, and don't forget the honey on top for added sweetness!

3/4 cup instant oatmeal

1 1/2 cups water

2 tablespoons almond milk

1/2 teaspoon lemon zest

1/8 teaspoon kosher salt

1/2 cup fresh blueberries

Honey, for serving

Add oatmeal, water, almond milk, lemon zest, and salt to the Skinny Mini. Stir, cover, and set to Cook.

At the end of the cycle, stir. Let sit, covered, for 5 minutes on Warm. To serve, top with blueberries and drizzle honey on top.

english muffin breakfast sandwich

For a quick and easy breakfast, you can use the Skinny Mini to both toast the English muffin and cook the egg at the same time. This breakfast sandwich tastes even better than the one from the coffee shop—and you can make it at home!

1 tablespoon butter

1 English muffin

1 egg

1 slice Canadian bacon or ham

1 slice Cheddar or American cheese

Butter each half of the English muffin, and put one muffin half in the bottom of the Skinny Mini. Crack the egg on the muffin half, add Canadian bacon, sliced cheese, and the top "lid" of the muffin. Cover, and set to Cook. When the cycle is complete, check the doneness of the egg; if desired, let it run through another Cook cycle. When the egg is cooked to your likeness, turn sandwich over and set to Cook to toast the other side of the muffin.

zucchini bread

Believe it or not, rice cookers can make fantastic quick breads. The trick is to make a drier dough—here I use yogurt instead of milk to give you the consistency you need. Add the yogurt a little bit at a time until the mixture is thick and just holds together, but is still on the dry side for a zucchini bread batter. As for the zucchini, grate it using an ordinary cheese grater, then drain it in a colander and blot the excess moisture with a paper towel.

1 cup pancake and baking mix, like Bisquick

1/4 cup granulated sugar

1/4 cup brown sugar, packed

1/8 teaspoon nutmeg

1 cup shredded zucchini, drained

2 tablespoons chopped walnuts

1 egg

1–2 tablespoons vanilla yogurt

In a medium bowl, combine baking mix, sugar, brown sugar, and nutmeg. Add the zucchini, walnuts, and egg and stir until well mixed. Add yogurt a little at a time, stirring after each addition, just until the mixture holds together, but is not overly moist.

Spread batter evenly in the Skinny Mini, cover, and set to Cook. When it switches to Warm, flip the bread using a spatula and set to Cook again. Remove once bread is cooked through (a toothpick inserted in the middle should come out clean).

spinach-mushroom omelet

You don't have to be a gourmet chef—or even be good with a frying pan—to make a great omelet in the Skinny Mini. Here's one of my favorite omelet recipes, featuring spinach and mushrooms.

1 teaspoon olive oil

$1/4$ cup shiitake, cremini, or other mushrooms, chopped

2 tablespoons finely chopped onion

4 eggs

$2/4$ cup milk

$1/4$ teaspoon kosher salt

$1/8$ teaspoon freshly ground black pepper

2 tablespoons chopped fresh spinach

2 tablespoons chopped tomatoes

$1/4$ cup shredded Cheddar cheese

1 teaspoon chopped fresh cilantro or parsley (optional), for serving

Add olive oil, mushrooms, and onions to the Skinny Mini. Stir to combine. Cover, set to Cook, and let cook for about 5 minutes. Separately, in a mixing bowl, whisk the eggs, milk, salt, and pepper until well combined. Add the egg mixture to the Skinny Mini, then top evenly with spinach, tomatoes, and cheese. Cover. When the Skinny Mini switches to Warm, switch it back to Cook and let it run through one more cycle. Leave on Warm until fully set if necessary. Garnish with cilantro or parsley if using before serving.

greek omelet

Get the taste of a Greek diner with this easy omelet featuring feta cheese.

4 eggs, beaten

$^3/_4$ cup milk

$^1/_4$ teaspoon kosher salt

$^1/_8$ teaspoon freshly ground black pepper

$^1/_8$ teaspoon dried oregano

2 tablespoons feta cheese, crumbled

2 tablespoons chopped fresh spinach

2 tablespoons chopped tomatoes

Chopped fresh parsley, for serving

Add all ingredients to the Skinny Mini, and stir to combine. Cover, set to Cook, then leave on Warm until fully set. Top with parsley before serving.

chilaquiles

Although nachos have Mexican origins, you're much more likely to see them at an American table than one south of the border. Chilaquiles are the true Latin cousins of American nachos. Instead of softening the chips with runny cheese, however, they're softened with salsa and a bit of broth. Use fresh tortilla chips from a Mexican restaurant, or crispy pita chips, to make sure they're thick enough to hold up to the sauce. Then top with a fried egg for a truly authentic touch!

2 tablespoons chicken stock, warmed

1 cup fresh tortilla chips or unseasoned kosher-salted pita chips, divided

1/2 cup your favorite salsa or Salsa Verde (page 25), divided

1/2 cup shredded chicken, divided (optional)

1 tablespoon finely chopped white onion

1/4 cup queso fresco, feta, or shredded Monterey Jack cheese

2 tablespoons sour cream

1 radish, thinly sliced, or 1/4 cup shredded lettuce

1 teaspoon chopped fresh cilantro

1 lime wedge

1 fried egg (optional)

Pour chicken stock into the Skinny Mini and top with half of chips. Then spread with half of the salsa and half the chicken (if using). Continue for one more layer until you have used all the chips and salsa. Cover and set to Cook for 6 minutes, until chips are warm and partially soft (queso fesco and feta will not melt). Stir, then pour onto serving plate and add onion, cheese, sour cream, radish or lettuce, and cilantro. Spritz the juice of the lime wedge over top. If desired, top with an egg fried in a skillet before serving.

quick fruit jam

This quick and easy fruit jam gives you the delectable taste of fresh jam without the hassle of canning and cooking the jam for hours. If it's too sweet for your taste, just add a pinch of baking soda once it's done.

1 cup frozen strawberries, blueberries, or other fruit, thawed

3/4 cup agave syrup

1 teaspoon water

1 (1-inch) strip orange peel, pith removed

Add all ingredients to the Skinny Mini and stir. Cover and set to Cook. After it switches to Warm, unplug the unit and let stand, covered, until cool. Remove orange peel before serving. Store leftovers in the refrigerator.

biscuits and honey

Buy a high quality kosher-salted butter and local honey.

2 rounds refrigerated biscuit dough

2 teaspoons honey

1 tablespoon high-quality kosher-salted butter

Place dough rounds on bottom of Skinny Mini. Cover and set to Cook. When done, top with butter and honey.

tasty
appetizers

Whether you're having a party or just feel like a fun snack on family movie night, the yummy appetizers in this section will have your friends and loved ones asking for more! Not only are they easy to make in a rice cooker, but thanks to the Skinny Mini's Warm setting, you don't have to worry about your hors d'oeuvres getting cold while you wait for your guests arrive.

steamed dumplings

Wonton wrappers are sold in many supermarkets these days, and they're great for stuffing with some Asian-inspired ingredients and steaming using the steamer insert of the Skinny Mini. This recipe uses a fragrant broth as the steaming liquid, which adds subtle flavor to the cabbage, mushroom, and carrot-filled dumplings. You can also add some ground chicken or pork for a meaty version.

$3/4$ cup chicken stock or water

1 slice lemon

1 slice lime

1 slice orange

2 scallions, chopped, divided

1 teaspoon crushed red pepper flakes

$1/2$ cup shredded Napa cabbage

$1/4$ cup coarsely grated carrots

2 tablespoons finely chopped mushrooms

1 teaspoon minced fresh ginger

1 small garlic clove, minced

1 teaspoon chopped chives

2 teaspoons soy sauce

1 teaspoon hoisin sauce

1 teaspoon sesame oil

1 egg, lightly beaten

$1/4$ teaspoon kosher salt

$1/8$ teaspoon freshly ground black pepper

Bowl of water, plus additional water for steamer

20 small wonton wrappers (thawed if frozen)

Nonstick cooking spray, for the steamer

Dipping sauce (such as soy sauce or ponzu), for serving

Add the stock, sliced fruit, half the scallions, and red pepper flakes to the Skinny Mini. Spray steamer insert with nonstick cooking spray and place the steamer insert on top.

In a large mixing bowl, add the remaining scallion, cabbage, carrots, mushrooms, ginger, garlic, chives, soy sauce, hoisin, sesame oil, egg, salt, and pepper. Lightly stir to combine.

Brush the edges of a wonton wrapper lightly with water. Place approximately two-thirds of a rounded tablespoon of the dumpling mixture in the center of the wrapper. Shape as desired. Place into steamer insert. Repeat until insert is full without overlapping. (You will have to cook in 2 or 3 batches.)

Cover and set to Cook. When the Skinny Mini switches to Warm, check for doneness, and if needed, set to run a second Cook cycle. Remove the dumplings to a heatproof platter and place in oven to keep warm. Repeat until all dumplings are cooked.

Serve dumplings with dipping sauce or pour broth over them to make a flavorful soup.

salsa verde

Salsa verde means "green sauce" in Spanish, and if you've never had it, you're in for a treat! Salsa verde gets its green color from tomatillos, which are small, green cousins of the tomato. Roast them up in the Skinny Mini and use this as a dip for chips or as a sauce in recipes like the easy enchiladas on page 96.

4 tomatillos, husked and washed

1/2 green bell pepper, chopped

1 serrano chile, seeds and ribs removed

2 cloves garlic, coarsely chopped

1/2 small red onion, chopped

2 tablespoons olive oil

1/2 cup chopped fresh cilantro

1/2 lime, juiced

1 tablespoon agave syrup

1/2 teaspoon kosher salt

1/2 teaspoon freshly ground black pepper

Add tomatillos, bell pepper, chile, garlic, onion, and olive oil to the Skinny Mini and toss until ingredients are coated in olive oil. Cover and set to Cook. Cook one cycle or until peppers are soft and tomatillos are shriveled. Place mixture in blender with remaining ingredients and blend until smooth.

pulled buffalo chicken dip

This is my go-to game-day dip—and once you serve it at a get-together, it might be your go-to, too, because everyone will ask you for it again! It's also a great use for rotisserie chicken—just shred the meat (thighs work best) with two forks or even your hands. If you want the dip to be less spicy, substitute sour cream for a portion of the wing sauce. You can also use ranch instead of blue cheese dressing!

1 cup shredded chicken

1/4 cup your favorite hot sauce

1 (8-ounce) package whipped cream cheese

1/4 cup blue cheese salad dressing

1/4 cup crumbled blue cheese

1/4 cup shredded Colby Jack cheese

Mix all ingredients in the Skinny Mini, and set to Cook. At the end of the cycle, stir and serve dip with corn chips, celery, bread, or crackers.

spinach-artichoke dip

Not only will spinach-artichoke dip always win raves at a party, you can even serve it over pasta for a decadent dinner.

1 (14-ounce) can quartered artichokes, chopped

$1/2$ (10-ounce) package frozen chopped spinach, thawed and drained

$1/2$ (8-ounce) package cream cheese, softened

$1/2$ cup mayonnaise

$1/2$ cup grated Parmesan cheese

1 garlic clove, minced

$1/2$ teaspoon kosher salt

$1/4$ teaspoon freshly ground black pepper

3 tablespoons dry white wine

Mix all ingredients thoroughly in the Skinny Mini. Set to Cook. When it switches to Warm, stir, and set to run through one more Cook cycle if not heated through. Serve with corn chips, bread, or crackers.

cheese fondue

Cheese fondue might be both the most delicious and most fun party appetizer you can have, but it's easy to burn the cheese on the stove, and hard to keep fondue warm. Not with the Skinny Mini! Add the cheese slowly and just melt and stir, then serve right in the unit while it's in Warm mode.

1 cup heavy cream

$^1/_2$ teaspoon ground dry mustard

$^1/_4$ teaspoon ground cayenne pepper

$^1/_4$ teaspoon nutmeg

$^1/_2$ teaspoon kosher salt

1 cup shredded Swiss cheese, at room temperature

1 cup shredded Cheddar cheese, at room temperature

$^1/_2$ cup shredded Monterey Jack cheese, at room temperature

Add the cream to the Skinny Mini, cover, and set to Cook. After 5 minutes, while stirring, add the mustard, cayenne, nutmeg, and salt. Cover again and allow to continue cooking until cream starts to steam and simmer slightly. Slowly start adding the cheeses by the handful, stirring well to incorporate. Switch to Warm cycle, cover, and stir occasionally until all cheese is melted and sauce is smooth. Serve with apple slices, bread cubes, celery, and carrots.

stuffed mini peppers

These stuffed mini bell peppers are not only delicious, they look great on a table of hors d'oeuvres—just make a few batches! People won't be able to resist picking one up to eat . . . and then eating a few more.

4 mini bell peppers, halved and seeded

1 tablespoon olive oil

$1/4$ cup shredded cooked chicken

1 tablespoon panko breadcrumbs

2 tablespoons Greek yogurt

$1/4$ teaspoon chopped fresh thyme

$1/2$ teaspoon chopped fresh cilantro

$1/8$ teaspoon minced garlic

$1/8$ teaspoon minced shallot

$1/4$ teaspoon kosher salt

$1/8$ teaspoon freshly ground black pepper

3 tablespoons shredded Monterey-jack and Cheddar cheese blend

Coat peppers in olive oil. In a medium bowl, combine olive oil, chicken, breadcrumbs, yogurt, thyme, cilantro, garlic, shallot, salt, and pepper. Stuff mixture into pepper halves and top with cheese. Place in Skinny Mini, in batches if necessary. Set to Cook. When the Skinny Mini switches to Warm, switch back to Cook and run through one more cycle, or until peppers are soft.

bacon-jalapeño cornbread

Looking for a way to make cornbread even more delicious? Bacon, as usual, does the trick. Combine it with spicy jalapeños and you have a cornbread that goes beyond side dish to something people will want to munch on before the main dish even comes out!

$1/2$ tablespoon vegetable oil

2 teaspoons finely chopped jalapeño peppers

1 (8.5 ounce) package cornbread and muffin mix

2 eggs

2 slices bacon, cooked and crumbled

$1/4$ cup sour cream

$1/4$ teaspoon freshly ground black pepper

$1/8$ teaspoon kosher salt

Add oil and jalapeños to Skinny Mini and toss to combine. Cover, and set to Cook, cooking until peppers are tender, about 5 minutes. Add remaining ingredients and mix well. Cover and cook for rest of Cook cycle. When the Skinny Mini switches to Warm, switch it back to Cook and let it run through one more cycle. Leave on Warm until toothpick inserted into the middle of the cornbread comes out clean. Turn upside down onto platter to serve.

spectacular sides

You may have purchased a rice cooker to make rice, but as you've learned by now, it can cook so much more! In this chapter you'll not only find dishes that take rice to a whole new level, but sides like polenta, couscous, and quinoa, and even a "rice" made from grated cauliflower that can open your eyes to all new culinary possibilities!

easy asian-style rice

This rice is a perfect accompaniment to stir-fries, chicken, or fish. You can even add whatever leftover meat or protein you have handy and make it into an easy meal on its own!

$3/4$ cup bamati rice, rinsed

3 tablespoons frozen vegetable medley

$1^1/2$ cups vegetable stock, chicken stock, or water

$1/2$ tablespoon butter or margarine

1 teaspoon soy sauce

$1/8$ teaspoon minced garlic

$1/8$ teaspoon minced ginger

$1/4$ teaspoon kosher salt

Add all ingredients to the Skinny Mini, and stir to mix well. Cover and set to Cook. After it switches to Warm, stir and let sit 5 more minutes before serving.

cilantro rice

Add a touch of something special to ordinary rice with this herby version that adds freshness to any meal. If you're not a fan of cilantro, use parsley, basil, or another garden herb instead. The addition of fresh corn during the summer months really makes this side dish shine!

$3/4$ cup long-grain rice, rinsed

$1^1/2$ cups chicken or vegetable stock

1 garlic clove

1 tablespoon diced onion

1 cup fresh sweet corn kernels (optional)

1 tablespoon chopped cilantro

1 teaspoon kosher salt

Add all ingredients to the Skinny Mini and stir to mix well. Cover and set to Cook. After it switches to the Warm setting, discard the garlic clove.

coconut rice with cashews

Many people think of coconut as a dessert food, but its sweetness pairs wonderfully with savory foods such as the long-grain rice in this recipe. Cashews give it even more decadence and a bit of crunch. Look for the coconut flakes, cardamom pods, and saffron at your local healthfood store.

1 cup long-grain rice, rinsed

1$^1/_2$ cups coconut milk

1/4 cup toasted, unsweetened coconut flakes

1/4 cup cashews

1 teaspoon kosher salt

2 whole cloves

1 black cardamom pod

1 thread saffron (optional)

Add all ingredients to the Skinny Mini and stir to mix well. Cover and set to Cook.

Fluff and mix lightly with a fork when finished. Remove cloves, cardamom, and saffron before serving.

mediterranean couscous

Couscous, a staple of Mediterranean cuisine, is a great way to mix up the everyday side-dish boredom of potatoes and rice. If you've never tried it, this is a quick and easy version with the traditional Mediterranean spices of cumin and coriander (actually the seeds of the cilantro plant!).

$3/4$ cup couscous

1 cup vegetable or chicken stock or water

$1/2$ teaspoon ground cumin

$1/2$ teaspoon ground coriander

$1/8$ teaspoon grated lemon zest

3 drops lemon juice

$1/4$ teaspoon kosher salt

$1/4$ teaspoon freshly ground black pepper

1 tablespoon chopped fresh cilantro leaves, for serving

Add all ingredients except the cilantro to the Skinny Mini and stir to mix well. Cover and set to Cook, stirring after the first 10 minutes. After the cooking cycle finishes, stir in the cilantro and serve.

couscous with raisins

Here's another delicious take on couscous, this time using dried fruit and nuts. This recipe uses raisins and pine nuts, but you can also use dried cranberries and almonds, apricots and pecans, or any combination you choose.

1 cup couscous

1 cup chicken stock

1 teaspoon butter

1 tablespoon chopped scallion

1 tablespoon chopped red bell pepper

1 tablespoon raisins

2 teaspoons pine nuts

1 teaspoon kosher salt

1 tablespoon chopped parsley, for serving

Add all ingredients except the parsley to the Skinny Mini and stir to mix well. Cover and set to Cook. After the cooking cycle finishes, top with parsley and serve.

creamy mac 'n' cheese

Way better than out of the box, this mac 'n' cheese is easy to make because the Skinny Mini does all the work for you—just throw the ingredients in and let it cook into a gooey, cheesy, delicious side that your family will beg for again and again.

3/4 cup macaroni pasta, rinsed

1 cup water

1/2 cup half-and-half, warmed

1/4 cup shredded Cheddar cheese, divided

1/4 cup crumbled queso fresco

1/4 cup grated Parmesan cheese

1/4 teaspoon kosher salt

1/4 teaspoon freshly ground black pepper

1/4 cup cherry or grape tomatoes, halved

Add pasta and water to the Skinny Mini, cover, and set to Cook. Cook until soft, checking after 10 minutes. Alternatively, boil water in a medium pot on the stove and cook pasta as directed on package. Drain pasta and add to the Skinny Mini.

In a separate bowl combine half-and-half, 3 tablespoons of Cheddar cheese, queso fresco, Parmesan cheese, salt, and pepper and mix until combined. Add cheese mixture to macaroni and stir. Top with tomatoes and remaining Cheddar cheese. Cover and leave on Warm for 30 minutes or until cheese sauce is melted.

parmesan polenta

Polenta is another side dish that is beloved throughout the world, but is not as well-known in the United States. This cornmeal-based side is wonderful alongside any meat, especially those that are full of robust flavor like sausages, ham, and roasts.

$1^2/_3$ cups water or stock

$^1/_2$ cup yellow cornmeal

$^1/_3$ cup milk

$^3/_4$ teaspoon kosher salt

$^1/_2$ teaspoon pepper

$^1/_3$ cup grated Parmesan cheese

1 tablespoon chopped parsley

1 tablespoon chopped rosemary

$^1/_2$ teaspoon minced garlic

Add stock to the Skinny Mini, cover, and set to Cook. When it comes to a boil (5–10 minutes), slowly add the cornmeal while stirring constantly. Add the remaining ingredients, stir, cover, and let it finish cooking. Let sit on warm until fully cooked, if necessary.

quinoa medley

If you've never tried quinoa (pronounced "KEEN-wah"), you're in for a treat! It has the nutty flavor of wild rice with the softness of barley, and has an incredible nutritional value, making it what many people call a "superfood." This recipe uses pine nuts, but you can swap them out for almonds, pistachios, or whatever you have on hand.

$3/4$ cup quinoa, rinsed

$1^1/2$ cups chicken stock

1 tablespoon butter

1 tablespoon toasted pine nuts

$1/2$ tablespoon dried cranberries

1 teaspoon kosher salt

1 teaspoon freshly ground black pepper

1 tablespoon chopped fresh parsley, for serving

Add all ingredients except the parsley to the Skinny Mini and stir to mix well. Cover and set to Cook. Cook for 2 cycles or until soft. Garnish with parsley.

cauliflower "rice"

Cauliflower "rice" is a godsend for anyone trying to cut back on carbs, but it's also a side dish that's addictingly delicious in its own right. Use a food processor to quickly chop the cauliflower into rice-sized bits, or simply use a cheese grater.

1 cup shredded cauliflower

1 teaspoon chopped fresh thyme

3/4 teaspoon chopped fresh parsley

1/4 teaspoon minced garlic

1 teaspoon minced shallot

1/4 cup vegetable stock

1/4 teaspoon kosher salt

1/8 teaspoon freshly ground black pepper

2 drops fresh lemon juice

Add all ingredients except the lemon juice to the Skinny Mini and stir to mix well. Cover and set to Cook. Stir again after 10 minutes, cover, and allow to complete the cooking cycle. If you want the cauliflower to be even softer, add a little more stock and set for a second Cook cycle. Stir in the lemon juice just before serving.

creamed spinach

Creamed spinach is a Southern dish, and once you eat the leafy green this way, you'll never want it prepared any other way! Best of all, it's super easy to make in the Skinny Mini.

1 cup whole milk, at room temperature

1 tablespoon cornstarch

2 cups frozen chopped spinach, thawed and water pressed out

1 tablespoon butter, melted

1/4 teaspoon ground nutmeg

1/4 teaspoon ground mustard

1 teaspoon kosher salt

In a cup mix milk and cornstarch until lumps dissolve. Add the spinach, butter, nutmeg, mustard, and salt to the Skinny Mini and stir to combine. Stir the milk mixture into the spinach mixture. Cover and set to Cook.

edamame and corn succotash

Succotash is another Southern dish that goes perfectly with any meal. It's traditionally made with lima beans, but I love to use snappy edamame (soybeans) instead, along with tasty black beans. Make sure to use a high-quality frozen corn: go for a bag that doesn't have frost on it and doesn't feel like a brick when you pick it up, which can be a sign that the corn has thawed and refrozen while en route to the store.

$^1/_2$ cup frozen corn kernels, thawed

$^1/_2$ cup frozen edamame or lima beans, thawed

$^1/_4$ cup drained black beans

1 teaspoon minced garlic

1 tablespoon minced shallots

1 cup vegetable broth or water

2 tablespoons chopped parsley

1 tablespoon chopped cilantro

Add all ingredients to the Skinny Mini and stir to mix well. Cover and set to Cook, stirring after 5 minutes. Serve when the cooking cycle is complete.

steamed asparagus

Sometimes, the most delicious side dishes are the simplest ones. The steamer insert of the Skinny Mini is perfect for steaming fresh spring asparagus or any other vegetable you find at your farmers market.

1 cup water

$1/2$ bunch asparagus

$1/2$ teaspoon kosher salt

$1/2$ teaspoon freshly ground black pepper

1 teaspoon butter

Add water to the Skinny Mini, and place the steamer basket on top. Add the asparagus, season with salt and pepper, and dot with butter. Cover and set to Cook until asparagus is bright green and tender but still crispy, about one cycle.

steamed vegetable timbale

The French "timbale" may sound impressive, but it's actually easy to make (especially in the Skinny Mini). Sort of like a lasagna where most of the layers are vegetables, timbales usually feature eggplant. Make sure to salt the slices and let them drain to remove bitterness and excess moisture.

$1/4$ eggplant, sliced

1 zucchini, sliced

2 small red potatoes, sliced

1 medium tomato, sliced and patted dry, divided

1 teaspoon chopped fresh oregano

$1/4$ cup olive oil

1 cup water

$1/4$ cup grated Parmesan cheese, divided

Kosher salt and freshly ground black pepper to taste

Toss eggplant with salt and allow to drain for at least 30 minutes to remove bitterness. Then rinse under cold water and pat dry.

Season remaining vegetable slices with salt and pepper to taste. Toss all vegetables, including eggplant, with oregano and olive oil until well coated.

Add water to the Skinny Mini and place the steamer insert on top. Starting with the potatoes, place the slices in the bottom of the steamer insert, and sprinkle with Parmesan cheese; next, add the eggplant, half of the tomatoes, and more Parmesan cheese; lastly add the zucchini, finishing with the remaining cheese and tomatoes. Cover and steam for 1–2 Cook cycles (about 20 minutes) or until tender. Serve while hot.

easy soups & sandwiches

Thanks to its Warm setting, the Skinny Mini is ideal for cooking soups, because you don't have to worry about them going cold before you serve them. But did you know you can make hot sandwiches in it, too?

homestyle chicken soup

Chicken soup is a must-have for cold winter days, sick family members, or anytime you need a comfort food. If you're in a hurry, just use a vegetable medley from the frozen foods section of your supermarket. And of course, whatever veggies you have in your crisper drawer always work in this versatile classic. I've included my favorite blend of vegetables to create a hearty, rustic flavor.

$1^3/_4$ cups chicken broth

$1/_4$ cup frozen vegetable medley or leftover vegetables

2 tablespoons finely chopped onion

$1/_4$ cup chopped cooked chicken

1 teaspoon ground cumin

$1/_2$ teaspoon paprika

$1/_4$ teaspoon ground coriander

$1/_2$ tablespoon chopped fresh parsley

1 teaspoon kosher salt

$1/_8$ teaspoon freshly ground black pepper

$1/_4$ teaspoon cayenne pepper (optional)

$1/_4$ cup small pasta, cooked

Add all ingredients to the Skinny Mini, cover, and set to Cook. When it switches to Warm, add cooked pasta and serve.

easy french onion soup

This quick-and-easy take on the classic onion soup is best with Vidalias—short, squat onions that are on the sweet side. Top the soup off with cheesy toast and it's hard to resist.

$^1/_2$ tablespoon vegetable oil

$^1/_2$ cup thinly sliced Vidalia onions

1 small garlic clove, peeled

$^1/_2$ teaspoon beef bouillon granules

$1^1/_2$ cups beef stock

1 slice Swiss cheese

1 slice French bread

Kosher salt and freshly ground pepper to taste

Place oil, onions, garlic, and bouillon in the Skinny Mini. Cover and set to Cook. After one cycle, stir, and add the beef stock. Cover and set to Cook again and continue cooking for 15 minutes. While the soup is cooking, put cheese on top of bread, and place in toaster oven or oven on broil until bread is toasted and cheese is melted, about 30–60 seconds. Taste the soup and add salt and pepper to taste. Remove garlic clove. Float the bread in the soup, allowing it to soak for a moment before serving.

warming lentil soup

In some parts of the world, lentils are part of practically every meal. A cousin of beans, they have an almost-nutty flavor that makes them perfect for a hearty soup. If you have some homemade chicken stock, use that instead of vegetable stock.

1 (15-ounce) can lentils, drained

$1^3/4$ cups vegetable broth

$1/4$ cup diced potatoes

1 tablespoon finely chopped celery

1 tablespoon finely chopped carrot

2 tablespoons finely chopped onion

1 garlic clove, minced

1 teaspoon ground cumin

1 teaspoon ground coriander

$1/2$ teaspoon paprika

1 teaspoon kosher salt

$1/2$ teaspoon freshly ground black pepper

1 teaspoon freshly chopped cilantro, for garnish

Add all ingredients except the cilantro to the Skinny Mini and mix well. Cover and set to Cook. When it switches to Warm, switch it back to Cook and let it run through one more cycle, or until broth is hot and potatoes are soft.

tomato and basil soup

If you love tomato soup, you'll adore this version with basil. Eat it with the grilled cheese sandwich with tomato on page 78!

1 tablespoon vegetable or olive oil

1/2 small yellow onion, chopped

1 garlic clove, halved

1 (14.5-ounce) can fire-roasted tomatoes

1 cup chicken broth

1 tablespoon tomato paste

2 tablespoons freshly chopped basil

Kosher salt and freshly ground black pepper to taste

1 tablespoon Greek yogurt or sour cream (optional)

Heat oil in small pan on stove over medium-high heat. When oil is hot, add onion and garlic. Heat, stirring occasionally, until onion and garlic are soft, about 5 minutes.

Transfer mixture to blender along with tomatoes, chicken broth, tomato paste, basil, and salt and pepper to taste. Blend until smooth.

Add puree to Skinny Mini, cover, and set to Cook one cycle, or until heated through. Top with Greek yogurt or sour cream.

beef vegetable soup

This is another recipe that's great for using up whatever veggies you have on hand, whether they're the frozen variety from the supermarket or the mixture of potatoes, celery, carrot, and onion I use here. Make sure to cook the soup until the beef becomes tender—it will be pretty tough until all of a sudden it will be mouthwateringly fall-apart delicious, and well worth the wait.

1 tablespoon vegetable oil

$1/4$ pound beef stew meat, cubed

$1^3/4$ cups beef broth

2 teaspoons Worcestershire sauce

$1/4$ cup diced potatoes

1 tablespoon finely chopped celery

1 tablespoon finely chopped carrot

2 tablespoons finely chopped onion

1 garlic clove, minced

1 bay leaf

1 teaspoon paprika

1 teaspoon kosher salt

1 teaspoon freshly ground black pepper

Heat oil in a small pan on stove over medium-high heat. Add beef cubes and brown on one side for 2–4 minutes, then turn. Cook, stirring occasionally, until browned on all sides, about 6–8 minutes more.

Add beef to Skinny Mini along with remaining ingredients and stir to combine. Cover and set to Cook. When it switches to Warm, switch it back to Cook and let it run through one more cycle, or until broth is hot and beef is tender. Remove bay leaf before serving.

black bean guiso

Guiso is a Latin stew. This version, with a black bean base, is easy to make in the Skinny Mini.

1 (15.5-ounce) can black beans with liquid

$1/2$ carrot, diced

$1/4$ red bell pepper, diced

$1/2$ small yellow onion, diced

$1/2$ teaspoon minced garlic

$1/2$ teaspoon minced fresh jalapeño

2 tablespoons diced onion

$1/2$ teaspoon ground cumin

$1/2$ teaspoon kosher salt

$1/4$ teaspoon crushed red pepper flakes

$1/2$ cup rice, cooked, for serving

Add all ingredients to the Skinny Mini and stir to combine. Cover and set to Cook. After 5 minutes, stir again, then let the Skinny Mini finish the cooking cycle. Serve with rice.

grilled cheese sandwich with tomatoes

Believe it or not, you can make a great grilled cheese sandwich in a rice cooker! I love this version with tomatoes—add bacon for a special treat. Keep an eye out at the grocery store for smaller breads, which will fit better in the Skinny Mini (Pepperidge Farm brand fits perfectly!).

2 slices sandwich bread

1 teaspoon softened butter

3 slices pepper Jack cheese

2 thin slices tomato

3 slices bacon, cooked (optional)

Lightly butter one side of each slice of bread. Place one slice of bread, butter side down, in the Skinny Mini, add cheese, then tomato slices, and bacon if using. Top with bread, butter side up. Cover and set to Cook. When the cycle is finished, turn sandwich over and set to Cook for another cycle. Serve immediately.

philly cheesesteak sandwich

The ingredients of a true Philly cheesesteak have long been debated (especially what kind of cheese to use). I like mine with chopped green bell pepper and onion and American cheese. I also like mine cooked in the Skinny Mini—build the sandwich right inside and it's ready to go once the cheese is melted.

1 kaiser roll, halved, or a sturdy burger bun

$1/4$ pound sliced roast beef, roughly chopped

2 tablespoons chopped green bell pepper

2 tablespoons chopped white onion

1 slice American, provolone, or Cheddar cheese

Place bottom half of kaiser roll in Skinny Mini, then top with roast beef, bell pepper, onion, cheese, and top half of roll. Cover and set to Cook. When cycle is finished, set to Cook for another cycle, or until cheese is melted and onions and peppers are tender. Leave on Warm until ready to eat.

delicious dinners

Add some meat to rice or another grain and there are thousands of dinners you can make in the Skinny Mini. But include the Skinny Mini's steamer insert and the possibilities are endless! In this chapter you'll find Peruvian-style fish, tacos and enchiladas, mushroom ragu, and more.

steamed mussels with white wine sauce

Mussels are wonderful dinnertime treat, and they couldn't be easier to make, especially in the Skinny Mini. Make a batch of French fries or get a loaf of crusty bread to sop up the delicious broth while you eat them!

1 teaspoon minced shallots

1 clove garlic, minced

1 sprig fresh thyme

$^1/_2$ cup dry white wine

Juice of $^1/_2$ lemon

$^1/_4$ cup chicken stock

$^1/_8$ teaspoon crushed red pepper flakes

1 teaspoon butter

$1^1/_2$ cups fresh mussels, cleaned

2 tablespoons chopped flat-leaf parsley, for garnish

Bread or French fries, for serving

Add all ingredients except the mussels and parsley in the bottom of the Skinny Mini. Place the steamer insert on top and add the mussels. Cover and set to Cook until all mussels are opened, 7–10 minutes. Then cook an additional 3 minutes after they open.

Place the mussels in a bowl and top with the broth. Sprinkle with fresh parsley and serve while hot with plenty of country bread or French fries.

lemon butter tilapia

The richness of butter and the tartness of lemon pair perfectly with fish, and this delicious Lemon Butter Tilapia is no exception. Better yet, with the steamer insert of the Skinny Mini, you can cook both the sauce and the fish at the same time!

3/4 cup white wine

1/4 cup water

1 tablespoon heavy cream

1 teaspoon capers

1/2 teaspoon kosher salt

1/2 teaspoon freshly ground black pepper

2 slices lemon

1 (approximately 6-ounce) tilapia fillet

1 (6-ounce) jar artichoke hearts, drained

1 tablespoon butter

Juice and zest of a lemon wedge, for serving

Add wine, water, cream, capers, salt, and pepper to Skinny Mini and stir. Place the steamer insert on top, and place the lemon slices, then tilapia, and then artichokes inside. Top with butter. Cover and set to Cook. Keep the Skinny Mini on Warm until fish is flaky and opaque.

Remove artichokes and fish. Stir sauce and pour over fish and artichokes. Top with lemon juice and zest.

peruvian-style white fish

This fish with Peruvian-style seasonings is one of my favorite ways to prepare white fish like halibut or cod. Complement it with one of the rices from the Spectacular Sides chapter, or with simple white rice.

1 teaspoon minced garlic

1 teaspoon grated fresh ginger

1 tablespoon light soy sauce

1 tablespoon coconut oil

1/8 teaspoon sugar

1/8 teaspoon kosher salt

1/8 teaspoon freshly ground black pepper

1 (5-ounce) skinless white fish fillet (such as halibut or cod)

1 cup water

2 slices lemon

1/4 jalapeño pepper, thinly sliced

2 scallions, chopped

Chopped cilantro, for garnish

In a small bowl mix together the garlic, ginger, soy sauce, oil, sugar, salt, and pepper until well combined. Add the fish and coat well with this mixture.

Add the water to the Skinny Mini and place the steamer insert on top. Place the lemon slices in the bottom of the steamer insert, followed by the fish. Sprinkle with scallions and jalapeño. Cover and set to Cook, until fish reaches desired level of doneness (setting for another Cook cycle if needed), about 20 minutes in total. Serve topped with fresh cilantro.

asian-inspired salmon

This salmon steamed with ginger, garlic, and touch of sesame oil is perfect with rice and some stir-fried vegetables.

3/4 cup water

1 teaspoon minced garlic

1 teaspoon minced ginger

2 scallions, chopped, divided

1/8 teaspoon toasted sesame oil

2 slices lemon

1 (approximately 6-ounce) salmon fillet

Add the water, garlic, ginger, half the chopped scallion, and sesame oil to the Skinny Mini. Add steamer insert and place lemon slices and then salmon inside. Cover and set to Cook. After one cycle, keep on Warm until salmon reaches desired level of doneness, about 15–25 minutes total cooking time. Remove fish and top with a bit of broth, if desired, and remaining scallion before serving.

shrimp with spicy broccoli rabe

Broccoli rabe is a unique vegetable with a strong, pleasant green flavor that holds up nicely to spice. I love pairing it with shrimp, like in this zesty dish.

1 cup white wine

$^1/_4$ cup water

1 teaspoon crushed red pepper flakes

1 small garlic clove, minced

$^1/_4$ pound fresh shrimp, peeled and deveined

$^1/_2$ cup chopped broccoli rabe

Kosher salt and freshly ground black pepper to taste

Bread or pasta, for serving

Add the wine, water, and red pepper flakes to the Skinny Mini. Place the steamer insert on top and add the shrimp and broccoli rabe. Cover and set to Cook, until broccoli rabe is tender and shrimp are opaque, about 15 minutes. Add salt and pepper to taste. Serve immediately with the wine broth and crusty bread or pasta.

barbecue shrimp

Grab a tub of coleslaw and serve it with this easy-to-make weeknight dinner that will mix up your usual chicken, chicken, chicken, beef routine.

1 tablespoon butter, melted

2 tablespoons your favorite barbecue sauce

1 tablespoon chopped chives

1/2 pound frozen shrimp, thawed

1 cup frozen corn

1/2 cup water

1 tablespoon chopped cilantro, parsley, or thyme leaves

In a mixing bowl, stir together the melted butter, barbecue sauce, and chives. Toss the shrimp in the sauce. Place corn and water in the Skinny Mini, add the shrimp mixture on top, cover, and set to Cook. When the cycle finishes, stir, top with herbs and serve immediately.

garlicky shrimp tacos

In Venezuela, we would call the filling for these flavorful tacos *gambas al ajillo*, or shrimp with garlic. If you don't have homemade salsa, chop up some tomatoes to bring out the freshness of the shrimp.

1 tablespoon butter

1 tablespoon olive oil

1 tablespoon chopped fresh parsley

2 small garlic cloves, minced

$1/2$ pound fresh shrimp, peeled and deveined

Tortillas, salsa, and lime wedges for serving

Place butter, olive oil, parsley, garlic, and shrimp in the Skinny Mini. Cover and set to Cook. Stir once butter is melted, about 5 minutes. After one cooking cycle, check to see if shrimp are opaque. If not, set to Cook again, checking regularly until they are done.

Serve on tortillas with salsa and a squeeze of lime juice.

chicken enchiladas

Anytime I have leftover chicken on hand, I always think of enchiladas. Pull the chicken with your fingers or two forks, then mix with the Salsa Verde from page 25 and top with cheese. What could be more delicious?

1 cup Salsa Verde (see page 25), divided

3/4 cup cooked chicken, pulled

1/2 cup shredded Monterrey-jack or Cheddar cheese

3 small corn tortillas

Sour cream and cilantro for garnish

In a medium bowl, combine ½ cup salsa verde and chicken. Divide mixture among tortillas.

Evenly spread ¼ cup salsa verde in the bottom of the Skinny Mini. Roll up each tortilla, then place seam-side down in Skinny Mini and top with cheese. Cover and set to Cook until cheese is melted and enchiladas are heated through, about two cycles. Top with remaining salsa verde, sour cream, and cilantro.

arroz con pollo

Arroz con Pollo, or chicken with rice, is a longstanding tradition in many Latin cuisines. Here's my take, Skinny Mini–style.

$3/4$ cup long-grain white rice, rinsed

1 cup chicken stock

$1/4$ cup chopped cooked chicken

1 tablespoon diced onion

1 clove garlic, peeled

1 tablespoon diced red bell pepper

1 teaspoon paprika

1 teaspoon minced ginger

$1/4$ teaspoon ground cumin

1 teaspoon kosher salt

Add all ingredients to the Skinny Mini and stir to combine. Cover and set to Cook.

Discard garlic clove if desired before serving.

orzo with chicken and feta

This fresh-tasting orzo dish is great for summer evenings and even picnics! It's also an ideal go-to for leftover chicken.

$3/4$ cup orzo

$1^1/_2$ cups water

1 tablespoon olive oil

$1/_2$ cup chopped cooked chicken

$1/_4$ cup crumbled feta cheese

$1/_4$ cup grape or cherry tomatoes, halved

$1/_2$ teaspoon dried oregano or basil

1 teaspoon kosher salt

1 teaspoon freshly ground black pepper

Add orzo and water to the Skinny Mini. Cover and set to Cook. Once it switches to Warm and the orzo is soft, drain and rinse with the pasta with cold water. In a small bowl, stir together the pasta and remaining ingredients.

meatballs in sauce

This simple meatball dish couldn't be easier. Serve over pasta or, if you're trying to eat fewer carbs, just enjoy as is.

1 (15-ounce) can tomato sauce

$1/2$ of 1 (14.5-ounce) can diced tomatoes with garlic

1 teaspoon dried oregano

1 teaspoon dried basil

$1/2$ teaspoon dried thyme

$1/8$ teaspoon paprika

$1/2$ teaspoon kosher salt

$1/2$ teaspoon freshly ground black pepper

$1/2$ of 1 (12-ounce) package refrigerated meatballs (or frozen meatballs, thawed)

Pasta or bread, for serving

Add all ingredients except meatballs to the Skinny Mini and stir. Add meatballs, cover, and set to Cook. Cook for 20 minutes, stirring frequently. Serve over pasta or with bread.

down-home meatloaf pie

Sometimes you get a craving that only meatloaf can satisfy! The Skinny Mini version comes out looking like a personal pie.

½ pound ground beef

¼ cup minced onion

¼ cup minced green bell pepper

1 teaspoon Worcestershire sauce

1 teaspoon minced garlic

2 tablespoons breadcrumbs

1 egg, beaten

½ teaspoon kosher salt

¼ teaspoon freshly ground black pepper

1 tablespoon ketchup

1–2 teaspoons brown sugar

In a medium bowl, mix ground beef, onion, bell pepper, Worcestershire sauce, garlic, breadcrumbs, egg, salt, and pepper until combined. Push the mixture into the bottom of the Skinny Mini, cover, and set to Cook. When the cycle finishes, turn meatloaf over with a spatula and set to Cook again. At the end of the second cycle, check for doneness, and add another cycle if needed. Mix together the ketchup and brown sugar, adding more brown sugar if you like a sweeter taste. Spread mixture over the top of the meatloaf and let rest for 5 minutes on Warm before serving.

ham and peas

Ham and peas are a perfect pair, which is why they've been served together pretty much as long as peas have been grown. Get the best-quality ham you can find at your market's deli counter to make this quick and easy meal that's great on its own or over buttered pasta.

$1^1/_2$ cups frozen peas

$^1/_4$ teaspoon kosher salt

$^1/_4$ teaspoon freshly ground black pepper

1 clove garlic, minced

3 tablespoons olive oil

1 cup water

$^1/_4$ pound serrano ham, sliced

Place the peas in a bowl; add the salt, pepper, garlic, and olive oil, and stir to combine. Add water to the Skinny Mini and place the steamer insert on top. Pour the peas into the steamer insert. Cover and set to Cook for 10 to 15 minutes or until done. Add the ham, toss, and serve.

three-mushroom ragu

Who needs meat when you have mushrooms? This rich and hearty meal contains three different kinds of mushrooms—I prefer button, cremini, and shiitake, but experiment with different kinds to get different tastes.

1 cup button mushrooms, chopped

1/2 cup cremini mushrooms, chopped

1/2 cup shiitake mushrooms, chopped

1 tablespoon butter

1 teaspoon minced garlic

1 tablespoon chopped parsley

1/4 cup dry white wine

1 teaspoon kosher salt

1/2 teaspoon crushed red pepper flakes

1/4 cup beef or vegetable stock

Add all ingredients to the Skinny Mini and stir to combine. Cover and set to Cook, stirring after 5 minutes. Allow the Skinny Mini to finish the Cook cycle. Serve over pasta or rice.

zucchini noodle spaghetti

I don't always recommend spending money on kitchen gadgets, but one I can't get enough of is the spiralizer, which you can use to turn vegetables like zucchini into spaghetti-like noodles. Not only does it make for a unique dish, it completely cuts out the carbs of traditional spaghetti!

1 medium zucchini, spiralized or cut into thin strips

1/4 teaspoon dried thyme

1/4 teaspoon dried oregano

1/4 teaspoon dried basil

2 tablespoons extra virgin olive oil

1/2 teaspoon kosher salt

1/4 teaspoon freshly ground black pepper

2 cups water

1/2 cup cherry or grape tomatoes, halved

1/4 cup feta cheese

In a small bowl, toss together the zucchini noodles, herbs, oil, salt, and pepper. Add water to the Skinny Mini and place the steamer insert on top. Add the seasoned zucchini. Cover and set to Cook for 10 minutes or until tender. Toss with tomatoes and feta. Keep on Warm until serving.

delectable desserts & drinks

Don't put away your Skinny Mini just yet! These after-dinner delights are great for putting into your rice cooker while you eat dinner; they'll be done by the time you are! And with the Warm setting, they'll stay just-out-of-the-oven warm until you're ready to enjoy them.

classic hot chocolate

What's better than a hot chocolate on a cold night (especially if there's a fireplace)? The Skinny Mini is perfect for making this classic concoction because you don't have to worry about overheating the milk. Just add the ingredients, flick the switch, and wait for it to warm!

2 tablespoons unsweetened cocoa powder

1½ tablespoons sugar

1 cup whole milk, divided

¼ teaspoon vanilla extract

2 tablespoons whipped cream, for serving

1 pip (section) chocolate bar, for serving

Add cocoa powder, sugar, and 2 tablespoons milk to the Skinny Mini. Whisk ingredients together, cover, and set to Cook, whisking once or twice during cook time. Once cocoa and sugar are dissolved (about 5 minutes), whisk in the rest of the milk and vanilla extract, and set to Warm.

When heated through (about 15 minutes), pour into mug and add whipped cream. Using a vegetable peeler, peel off shavings of chocolate and sprinkle on top for garnish.

white chocolate–peppermint hot chocolate

This hot chocolate uses melted white chocolate chips and a touch of peppermint for a unique and tasty beverage that's best enjoyed with a plate of Christmas cookies!

$1/4$ cup white chocolate chips

1 cup whole milk, divided

$1/4$ teaspoon peppermint extract

2 tablespoons whipped cream, for serving

1 candy cane, for serving

Add white chocolate chips and 2 tablespoons milk to Skinny Mini. Cover and set to Cook, stirring occasionally during cook time. When chocolate is melted (about one Cook cycle), add remaining milk and peppermint extract. Whisk thoroughly, then set to Warm.

When heated through (about 15 minutes), pour into mug and add whipped cream. Add a candy cane for garnish.

simple horchata

Horchata is a super-popular drink in Latin countries—and once you taste it, you'll know why. It's refreshing yet homey, thanks to its combination of cinnamon and sugar. This version makes it easy by using rice milk instead of having to soak rice in water. Stir in a bit of instant ground espresso to make it a horchata latte!

1 cup water

1/2 cup sugar

1/4 teaspoon ground cinnamon

1 (64-ounce) carton rice milk

Add water, sugar, and cinnamon to the Skinny Mini. Cover and set to Cook. Cook until sugar dissolves, stirring occasionally, about 5 minutes. Allow mixture to cool for 10–15 minutes, then combine with rice milk in a pitcher. Stir until combined, then refrigerate for at least 1 hour. Serve with ice.

spiced apple cider

Take store-bought apple cider to the next level in this easy recipe that's perfect for winter nights.

1 cup apple cider or fresh apple juice

1 cinnamon stick

1 whole clove

2 ½-inch-wide slices lemon peel

1 ounce rum (optional)

Add apple cider, cinnamon, clove, and lemon peel to the Skinny Mini, cover, and set to Cook. When it switches to Warm, add rum if desired and let sit for 5 more minutes. Remove cinnamon stick, clove, and lemon peel before serving.

crustless cheesecake

Calling all cheesecake lovers! Making a cheesecake at home has never been easier than with this simple recipe for the Skinny Mini. Top it with your favorite berries, chocolate sauce, or a scoop of ice cream for a special treat!

1 (8-ounce) package cream cheese, softened

$^1/_4$ cup sugar

2 large eggs

$^3/_4$ cup heavy cream

1 teaspoon vanilla extract

2 tablespoons cornstarch

$^1/_8$ teaspoon kosher salt

2–3 strawberries, halved

In medium bowl, combine cream cheese and sugar. Beat on high with a hand mixer until smooth, about 30 seconds. Add eggs, one at a time, and beat until combined, about 30 seconds. Stir in cream, vanilla, cornstarch, and salt and mix until combined and fluffy, about 1 minute.

Pour mixture into Skinny Mini. Cover and set to Cook. When the Skinny Mini switches to Warm, set to Cook again. After 5 minutes of additional cooking time, check to see if the cheesecake has set (a toothpick inserted into the center should come out clean). Keep cooking until set. Remove with a spatula, allow to cool, and refrigerate overnight or for several hours before serving. Top with strawberries.

pineapple upside-down cake

Pineapple upside-down cakes are fun to make thanks to their ingenious top-first construction, but they're also delicious too! Who knew pineapple and cake went so well together?

2 tablespoons butter or margarine, melted

1/2 cup brown sugar, packed

1 (8-ounce) can pineapple slices in juice, drained, juice reserved

Water

1/2 of 1 (15.25-ounce) box yellow cake mix

1/2 tablespoon vegetable oil

1 egg

Pour melted butter into the Skinny Mini and spread evenly over bottom. Sprinkle evenly with brown sugar on top, then top with pineapple slices, pressing them into the sugar mixture.

Add water to reserved pineapple juice until you reach 1/3 cup. In large bowl, stir together liquid with cake mix, vegetable oil, and egg until just combined. Pour over pineapple slices.

Cover and set to Cook for 2–3 cycles, until cake is cooked through (a toothpick inserted into the center should come out clean). Flip onto a plate to serve.

orange-carrot cake

The fresh orange flavor in this carrot cake helps make it lighter and airier. Better yet, it's super-easy to make in the Skinny Mini!

1/2 of 1 (15.25-ounce) box yellow cake mix

1/4 cup orange juice

1/4 cup butter, softened

1/4 teaspoon ground cinnamon

1/8 teaspoon ground nutmeg

1 teaspoon vanilla extract

1 egg

1 large carrot, shredded

1 teaspoon orange zest

1/2 cup creamy-style cream cheese frosting

In a medium bowl, add all ingredients and whisk just until smooth (do not overmix). Add to the Skinny Mini and set to Cook for 2–3 cycles, until cake is cooked through (a toothpick inserted into the center should come out clean). Remove to wire rack and let cool completely before frosting and serving.

brownies à la mode

If you've ever craved brownies on a warm day, you'll love this simple recipe that doesn't require turning on your oven. Just use your favorite brownie mix and halve the recipe. (Make the second half tomorrow!)

$^1/_2$ of 1 (18-ounce) box your favorite brownie mix

Eggs, water, and oil according to brownie package directions

$^1/_4$ cup milk-chocolate chocolate chips

Ice cream and fresh berries (optional), for serving

In a large mixing bowl, combine brownie mix and half of eggs, water, and oil amounts listed on brownie package. Mix in chocolate chips.

Pour batter into the Skinny Mini and set to Cook. When it switches to Warm, switch back to Cook for at least one more cycle. Remove when brownies are set and a toothpick inserted in the middle comes out clean. Serve with a scoop of ice cream and fresh berries.

caramelized dessert apples

This decadent dessert tastes like apple pie without the crust. For best results, use a solid baking apple like Granny Smith, Honeycrisp, Fiji, Gala, or Cortland—or better yet, a mixture of two! Serve with vanilla ice cream with an extra sprinkling of cinnamon on the top with vanilla ice cream.

2 apples, peeled and cut into large chunks

2 tablespoons water

$1/4$ cup butter, melted

$1/4$ cup brown sugar, packed

1 teaspoon ground cinnamon

All ingredients in the Skinny Mini and mix to combine. Cover and set to Cook. Cook until apples are tender, about one Cook cycle.

poached spiced pears

This classy dessert may take a while, but almost all the time spent is in the Skinny Mini—meaning you can cook them while you eat dinner! A perfect finish to an elegant meal, these pears for two are sophisticated and, as a bonus, very low in calories!

$1^1/2$ cups red wine (such as pinot noir)

$1/4$ cup water

$1/2$ cup sugar

1 whole black peppercorn

1 whole clove

1 whole star anise

2 $1/2$-inch-wide strips lemon peel

1 cinnamon stick

2 ripe Bartlett or Bosc pears, peeled

2 scoops vanilla ice cream (optional, for serving)

$1/4$ teaspoon freshly grated nutmeg (optional, for serving)

2 mint sprigs (optional, for serving)

Add wine, water, sugar, peppercorn, clove, star anise, lemon peel, and cinnamon stick to the Skinny Mini. Cover and set to Cook, stirring occasionally once or twice during cooking time, until the sugar is dissolved and mixture has reduced slightly, about one cycle.

When the Skinny Mini switches to Warm, add the pears and set for another Cook cycle, cooking until the pears are tender and a paring knife easily slips into the center, about 15 minutes. Use a slotted spoon to transfer the pears to a small bowl and set aside.

Remove and discard the peppercorn, clove, anise, lemon peel, and cinnamon stick. Cover and set on Cook again for a total of two more Cook cycles, or until liquid is reduced by half and is the consistency of a thick syrup, about 30 minutes.

Return the pears to the thick poaching liquid and heat for 1 minute, basting the pears with the syrup. To serve, place pears on plates and then drizzle each portion with 2 tablespoons poaching syrup, and then top with a scoop of vanilla ice cream, a grating of nutmeg, and a mint sprig, if using.

raspberry bread pudding

This beautiful and refreshing dessert couldn't be easier to make in the Skinny Mini. If you don't have day-old bread, dry your bread out a bit by placing it in the oven on a baking sheet at 300°F for 5–10 minutes.

$1/2$ cup heavy cream

1 teaspoon dark rum

1 teaspoon water

$1/8$ teaspoon vanilla extract

1 large egg

3 tablespoons sugar

$1/8$ teaspoon kosher salt

3 slightly stale croissants, cut into 1-inch cubes

1 tablespoon white chocolate chips

$1/4$ cup fresh raspberries

In a large mixing bowl, stir together cream, rum, water, vanilla, eggs, sugar, and salt until sugar has dissolved. Submerge bread cubes in mixture and mix in chocolate chips and raspberries; let soak for 2 minutes. Pour mixture into the Skinny Mini. Cover and set to Cook until top springs back when touched lightly, about one Cook cycle.

cinnamon
rice pudding

If you've never tried rice pudding, you're in for a treat! Although rice might not seem like a natural dessert item at first, once you see how silky and creamy it becomes in pudding form, you'll love it! It tastes even better in this classic pairing with cinnamon.

1 cup short-grain rice, rinsed

1 cup cold water

$1/4$ teaspoon kosher salt

1 tablespoon butter, melted

2 tablespoons brown sugar, packed

$3/4$ cup whole milk

$1/4$ teaspoon vanilla extract

1 teaspoon cinnamon

Add rice, water, and salt to the Skinny Mini, cover, and set to Cook. Cook until it switches to Warm, about 15 minutes. Turn off Skinny Mini and let cool for 10 minutes.

Meanwhile in medium bowl, mix together melted butter and brown sugar. Then add milk, vanilla, and cinnamon and stir until sugar is dissolved. Add milk mixture to rice in Skinny Mini and stir until well combined. Cover and set to Warm until thickened, about 30 minutes.

chocolate fondue

This party classic couldn't be easier in the Skinny Mini—especially because its Warm feature makes it the perfect serving vessel! Grab some forks and dip anything that tastes good in this gooey chocolate sauce. Who needs a fondue pot?

1 cup heavy cream

1 teaspoon ground cinnamon

2^1/$_2$ cups dark chocolate chips

banana slices, pound cake, strawberries, marshmallows, potato chips, or anything you like!

Add the cream to the Skinny Mini, cover, and set to Cook. After 5 minutes, while stirring constantly, add the cinnamon and begin adding the chocolate chips, about ½ cup at a time, making sure the ones just added are completely melted before adding more. Continue stirring until all chocolate has been added and melted. Set the Skinny Mini to Warm (covered), wait 5 minutes, and serve immediately.

index

SKINNY MINI COOKBOOK